THE BEST
DOGS
EVER

BEAGLES ARE THE BEST!

Elaine Landau

LERNER PUBLICATIONS COMPANY · MINNEAPOLIS

For Rocco Staino

Lerner Publications Company
A division of Lerner Publishing Group, Inc.
241 First Avenue North
Minneapolis, MN 55401 U.S.A.

Website address: www.lernerbooks.com

Library of Congress Cataloging-in-Publication Data

Landau, Elaine.
    Beagles are the best! / by Elaine Landau.
        p.   cm. – (The best dogs ever)
    Includes index.
     ISBN 978-1-58013-559-7 (lib. bdg. : alk. paper)
    1. Beagle (Dog breed)–Juvenile literature. I. Title.
    SF429.B3L34 2010
    636.7537–dc22   2008046789

Manufactured in the United States of America
1 2 3 4 5 6 – BP – 15 14 13 12 11 10

TABLE OF CONTENTS

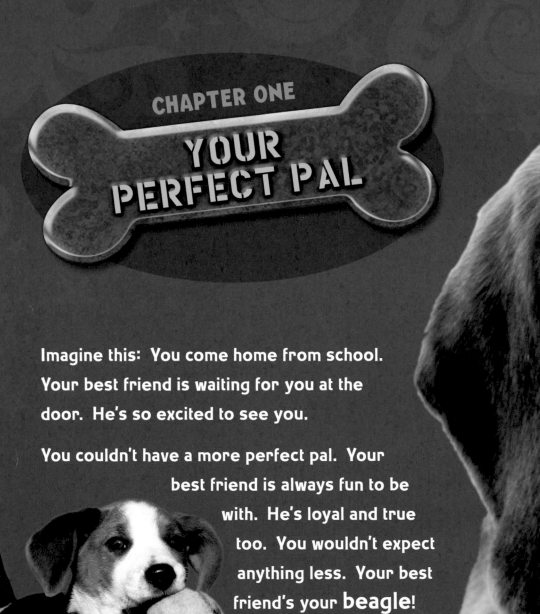

CHAPTER ONE
YOUR PERFECT PAL

Imagine this: You come home from school. Your best friend is waiting for you at the door. He's so excited to see you.

You couldn't have a more perfect pal. Your best friend is always fun to be with. He's loyal and true too. You wouldn't expect anything less. Your best friend's your **beagle**!

A Happy Dog

Beagles are happy, gentle, and friendly. These handsome pooches have soft, floppy ears. Their big eyes can melt your heart.

Beagles enjoy being around people. They are especially good with young children. Your dog may want to meet and greet all your guests.

WHAT TO CALL YOUR BEAGLE

Looking for a great name for your beagle? You might like some of these:

BUSTER   Dixie

Ernie

Maggie

Murphy   Cassie

SAM   ROCKY   LUCY

Missy

Is That Dog a Beagle?

Beagles come in two sizes. The smaller ones are between 10 and 13 inches (25 and 33 centimeters) tall at the shoulder. They weigh from 18 to 20 pounds (8 to 9 kilograms). That's about as much as two medium-sized rabbits.

Bigger beagles measure between 13 and 15 inches (33 to 38 cm) tall at the shoulder. These dogs can weigh up to 30 pounds (14 kg). That's about as much as two large house cats.

Most beagles are tricolor. This means their coats are three different colors. Tricolor beagles are usually white, black, and tan. But beagles can be other colors too.

Free Spirits

Beagles enjoy going places with their owners. They are often the merriest guests at family picnics and parties. Yet beagles don't cling to their owners. These dogs are curious about things. They like to explore. That makes them even more fun. Their owners think beagles are the best dogs ever!

Beagles like to go new places and visit people. They'll go anywhere with you!

CHAPTER TWO

WHAT A HOUND!

Beagles are super-sniffers. These dogs are great at picking up a scent. It's what they do best!

Beagles are hounds. Hounds are a type of dog that is often used for hunting. All hounds have an excellent sense of smell.

Beagles can follow scent trails left by animals in the grass.

THEY CAN TELL BY THE SMELL

Beagles have a much better sense of smell than people. This is partly because they have more scent receptors in their noses than people do.

Scent receptors are special cells used for smelling. People have about 5 million scent receptors in their noses. Beagles have about 220 million. That's quite a difference!

Hound Dog History

Hounds have helped people hunt for hundreds of years. By the 1800s, beagles were doing this in Great Britain. The dogs' keen noses helped them find rabbits and hares.

Many people moved to the United States from Great Britain. Some brought their beagles with them. Soon Americans hunted with these dogs too.

Some beagles helped hunters on horseback. This painting shows beagles helping hunters in Great Britain.

A working beagle barks after finding a package of meat at an airport.

Beagles Today

These days, beagles do more than hunt. Some help the U.S. government. These beagles work at airports. Their job is to sniff people's bags. They are looking for fruits, plants, and meats that should not be brought into the country. These items could contain harmful insects and diseases.

BEAGLES SAVE BUILDINGS!

Termites are a big problem for many homeowners. These insects eat wood. They can destroy a house. But beagles can help protect houses from termites. How?

Beagles are terrific termite trackers. These dogs sniff out the termites' nesting places. Then pest control agents (people hired to remove insects and other pests from buildings) can remove the termites.

Dog Groups

The American Kennel Club (AKC) groups dogs by breed. Some of the AKC's groups include the sporting group, the working group, and the toy group. Beagles are in the hound group. (No surprises there!)

Basset hounds are part of the hound group—just like beagles!

This boxer belongs to the working group.

Springer spaniels, like this one, are in the sporting group.

Other dogs in the hound group are the basset hound and the bloodhound. The dachshund belongs to this group as well. That's the dog some say looks like a walking hot dog!

Dogs in the hound group do not look alike. But they do have one thing in common. Their great noses and ability to follow a trail impresses and amazes their human companions!

WHAT A WINNER!

The year 2008 was great for beagle lovers. A beagle named K-Run's Park Me in First won Best in Show at the Westminster Kennel Club Dog Show. The winner, also known as Uno, was the first beagle to ever receive this honor.

The crowd at the show really fell for Uno. When he won, they stood up and cheered. They chanted Uno's name. Uno loved all the attention. He looked like one happy hound that night!

Uno stands with his prize cup and trophy after winning Best in Show at the 2008 Westminster Kennel Club Dog Show.

CHAPTER THREE
THE RIGHT DOG FOR YOU

What's cuter than a baby? You might say a puppy. Beagle puppies are supersweet. It's easy to fall for those loving eyes and floppy ears.

But there are lots of cute puppies. Why get a beagle? Is a beagle your best bet? Some people adore beagles. Others have very different dream dogs.

Get Off the Couch

Are you a couch potato? Do you spend most
of your free time indoors? Young beagles
need lots of exercise. Some have quite a bit
of energy.

You'll need to take your beagle for at
least two twenty-minute walks a day.
Playing with your beagle is important
too. If the thought of this makes
you want to hide under the couch,
pass on getting a beagle.

Too Busy for a Beagle?

How busy are you? Does soccer or ballet take up much of your time? Would you rather play video games than play with a dog? Then a beagle may not be for you.

You may have heard of "people people." Those are people who like being around other people. Beagles are "people dogs." They like being around people too. Beagles don't do well alone. Don't get a beagle if no one's going to be with it.

Beagles get lonely when there's no one around to play with them.

Is That Music I Hear?

Some beagles do a lot of baying. Baying is a little like howling. It helps in hunting. A hunting beagle will bay when it finds a rabbit. That lets the hunter know where the rabbit is.

Yet what if you don't hunt and just want a pet? Well, beagles make great pets. But they were still bred to hunt. Your beagle may bay at a squirrel in a tree in your yard for hours. How would you feel about the baying? Would your neighbors feel the same way?

Patience, Please

If at first you don't succeed, try, try again. Have you ever heard that saying? You'll have to keep it in mind when training a beagle.

Beagles are not the easiest dogs to train. They are known to be a bit stubborn. They are also very smart and curious. They get bored easily during training time.

This doesn't mean you should give up. There are many well-trained beagles. You just need a lot of patience and love.

Young beagles like to chew on things. You will need to train your beagle not to chew on furniture or shoes.

CITY DOG OR COUNTRY DOG

Beagles live happily in both the city and the country. You'll find them in houses as well as apartments. A big beagle is still a small dog. It can fit in well just about anywhere.

You'll have many things to think about when deciding whether to get a beagle. These dogs often live for more than fifteen years. That's a long time. So you want to be sure that a beagle is the best new family member you can find.

If it is, you're in luck! You're going to have lots of fun. A warm, loving, new best friend is about to enter your life.

CHAPTER FOUR

THE HOMECOMING

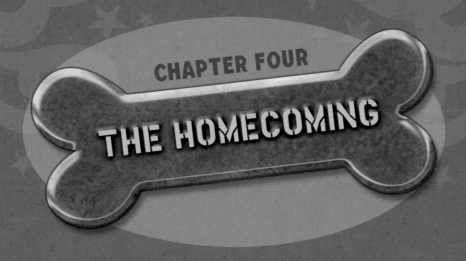

I'm thinking of a special day. Can you guess what day it is? It's better than a birthday. It's more fun than the last day of school. It's the day you bring your beagle home.

You'll want your beagle to feel at home right away. So be ready for your pet. Not sure what you'll need to welcome Fido to your family? This basic list is a great place to start:

collar

leash

tags (for identification)

dog food

food and water bowls

crates (one for when your pet travels by car and one for it to rest in at home)

treats (to be used in training)

toys

Your new beagle might enjoy sleeping in a cozy dog bed that's just his size.

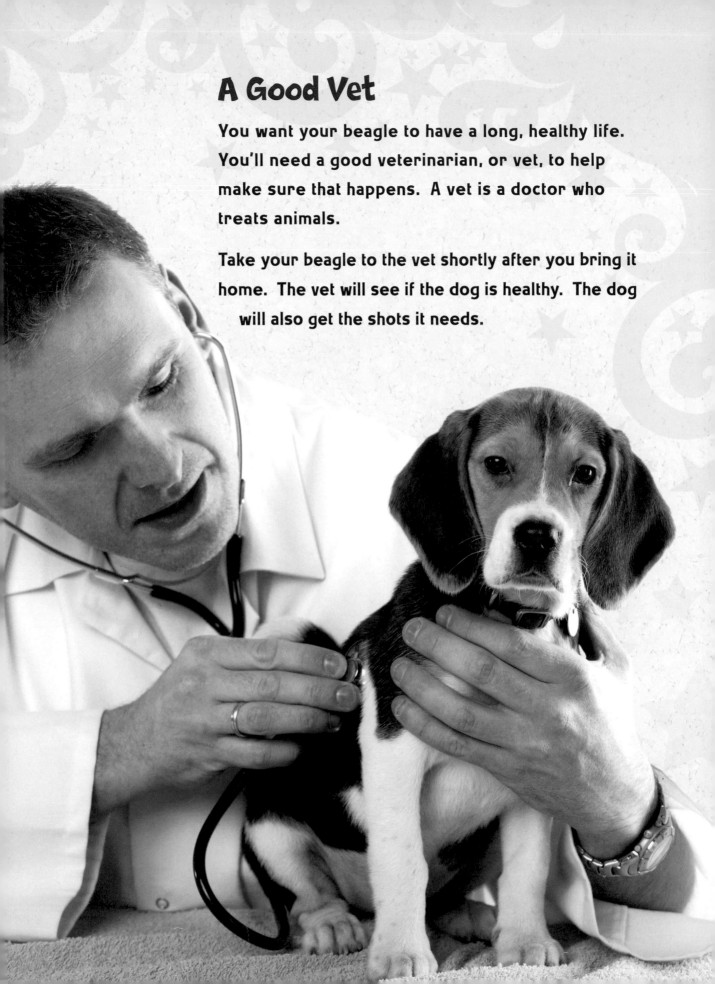

A Good Vet

You want your beagle to have a long, healthy life. You'll need a good veterinarian, or vet, to help make sure that happens. A vet is a doctor who treats animals.

Take your beagle to the vet shortly after you bring it home. The vet will see if the dog is healthy. The dog will also get the shots it needs.

Ask your vet any questions you have about caring for your dog. You can count on your vet for the right answers.

You'll be seeing the vet a lot. Your dog will need to get shots throughout its life. You'll also need to take your dog to the vet if it becomes ill.

If your beagle gets sick, the vet will take its temperature and listen to its heartbeat.

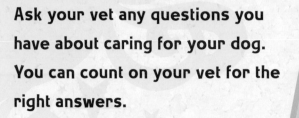

GOOD GROOMING

Both people and dogs should be well groomed. Brush your beagle twice a week. Clean its long, floppy ears weekly too.

Feeding Time!

Feed your dog a good-quality dog food. Ask your vet what food would be best. Do not give your beagle table scraps.

Beagles are big eaters. They love their food. This often leads to overeating. Beagles can easily become overweight. Don't give your dog too many doggie treats. Use treats only as rewards for good behavior.

NOT A WATCHDOG

Don't get a beagle for a watchdog. It won't work. These dogs are just too sweet and friendly. Don't count on your beagle to attack an intruder. The dog is more likely to lick him instead.

Up and Out with Your Beagle— Exercise Time!

Beagles need exercise. They don't like being inside all day. Since beagles are big eaters, exercise is important for them. It can help keep their weight down.

Walks with your beagle can be fun. But don't take your beagle out without a leash. You may be sorry if you do. Beagles can pick up a scent and take off. You can try calling your dog back if it runs away—but most beagles will keep following the scent.

Beagles can run for a long time before they tire out.

You can play ball or fetch with your beagle. You may even want to let your dog run free at times. Just be sure you do this in a fenced-in area—like a special park for dogs or a backyard with a fence. You don't want to lose your dog.

Leader of the Pack

Beagles are pack animals. They sometimes hunt in groups. Now your beagle is joining a new pack. It's your family.

To your dog, you're the leader of the pack. Your dog will depend on you for food, training, and love. Don't let your beagle down.

This pack of beagles is ready to go hunting.

Take time to be with your beagle. Your dog will be your best friend. Be your dog's best friend as well.

GLOSSARY

American Kennel Club (AKC): an organization that groups dogs by breed. The AKC also defines the characteristics of different breeds.

baying: a howling sound

breed: a particular type of dog. Dogs of the same breed have the same body shape and general features. *Breed* can also refer to producing puppies.

coat: a dog's fur

hound: a type of dog that is often used for hunting

hound group: a group of dogs that have a good sense of smell and are often used for hunting

pack: a group of animals or people

scent receptor: a special cell used for smelling

tricolor: three different colors. Most beagles' coats are tricolor.

veterinarian: a doctor who treats animals. Veterinarians are called vets for short.

FOR MORE INFORMATION

Books

Brecke, Nicole, and Patricia M. Stockland. *Dogs You Can Draw*. Minneapolis: Millbrook Press, 2010. This colorful book shows how to draw different kinds of dogs, including the beagle, and shares fun facts about each breed.

Mulvany, Martha. *The Story of the Beagle*. New York: PowerKids Press, 2000. This text describes the beagle's role as a hunter, pet, and working dog.

Murray, Julie. *Beagles*. Edina, MN: Abdo, 2002. This book offers an introduction to the beagle, including its history and proper care.

Stone, Lynn M. *Beagles*. Vero Beach, FL: Rourke, 2003. Read this book to learn more about the beagle's nature and how the breed was developed.

Websites

ASPCA Animaland
http://www.aspca.org/site/PageServer?pagename=kids_pc_home
Check out this website for helpful hints on caring for a dog and other pets.

Petpourri
http://www.avma.org/careforanimals/kidscorner
This page from the American Veterinary Medical Association includes fun games and activities to help you learn more about pet care.

Index

Photo Acknowledgments

The images in this book are used with the permission of: backgrounds © iStockphoto.com/Julie Fisher and © iStockphoto.com/Tomasz Adamczyk; © iStockphoto.com/Verity Johnson, p. 4; © Fotosmurf02/Dreamstime.com, pp. 4-5; © Index Stock Imagery/Photolibrary, p. 5; © Akira Matoba/SuperStock, p. 6; © age fotostock/SuperStock, pp. 6-7; © Purestock/Getty Images, pp. 8 (top), 28 (top); © Lochef/Dreamstime.com, p. 8 (bottom); © Michalnapartowicz/Dreamstime.com, p. 9; © Mdtrttcmd/Dreamstime.com, p. 10 (top); © After Samuel Henry Gordon Alken/The Bridgeman Art Library/Getty Images, pp. 10-11; AP Photo/Mike Derer, p. 11; © Jerry Shulman/SuperStock, pp. 12 (left), 12-13; © Isselee/Dreamstime.com, p. 12 (right); © Timothy A. Clary/AFP/Getty Images, p. 13; © iStockphoto.com/ronibgood56, p. 14; © Arthur Tilley/Taxi/Getty Images, p. 15; © Francis Miller/Time & Life Pictures/Getty Images, p. 16 (top); © Koki Iino/MIXA/Getty Images, p. 16 (bottom); © Juniors Bildarchiv/Photolibrary, pp. 16-17; © iStockphoto.com/Mariya Bibikova, p. 18; © iStockphoto.com/Martin Tanner, pp. 18-19; © DAJ/Getty Images, p. 19; © iStockphoto.com/Andrea Krause, p. 20; © Image Source/ZUMA Press, p. 21; © Tooties/Dreamstime.com, p. 22 (top); © Uturnpix/Dreamstime.com, p. 22 (second from top); © iStockphoto.com/orix3, p. 22 (second from bottom); © iStockphoto.com/Al Bello, p. 22 (bottom); © iStockphoto.com/Monika Wisniewska, pp. 22-23, 24-25; © iStockphoto.com/Willie B. Thomas, p. 24 (top); © iStockphoto.com/Ivan Solis, p. 24 (bottom); AP Photo/The Anderson Independent-Mail, Sefton Ipock, p. 26 (top); © iStockphoto.com/Ken Hurst, p. 26 (bottom); © Christopher Allan/Gallo Images/Getty Images, pp. 26-27; © Steve Shott/Dorling Kindersley/Getty Images, p. 28 (bottom); © Noel Hendrickson/Digital Vision/Getty Images, p. 29.

Front Cover: © Merro83/Dreamstime.com. Back Cover: © Isselee/Dreamstime.com